For Sam Oakley N.D.

For Alan and Annabel N.L.

J573.
49

THE COMMON GENET ON
THE OPPOSITE PAGE IS
Sniffing a big pile of POO.
YOU CAN FIND OUT WHY IF YOU
TURN TO PAGE 31.

First published 2004 by Walker Books Ltd, 87 Vauxhall Walk, London SE11 5HJ

10 9 8 7 6 5 4 3 2 1

Text © 2004 Nicola Davies   Illustrations © 2004 Neal Layton

The right of Nicola Davies and Neal Layton to be identified as author and illustrator respectively of this work has been asserted by them in accordance with the Copyright, Designs and Patents Act 1988

This book has been typeset in AT Arta

Printed in China

British Library Cataloguing in Publication Data: a catalogue record for this book is available from the British Library

ISBN 0-7445-8634-8 (hb)
ISBN 1-84428-751-3 (pb)

www.walkerbooks.co.uk

Poo

A Natural History of the Unmentionable

by **Nicola Davies**

illustrated by **Neal Layton**

WALKER BOOKS
AND SUBSIDIARIES
LONDON · BOSTON · SYDNEY · AUCKLAND

Grown-ups are shy about it…

Horses ignore it…

Dogs like to sniff it…

And babies do it in their nappies…

Poo, big jobs, number twos. Whatever you call it, faeces (to give it one of its proper names) are everywhere. We humans may find it revolting and embarrassing, but the truth is that all animals do poos of some sort. Or, to put it scientifically, all animals defecate. And the faeces that they make come in all shapes and sizes.

A TOUR OF POO

Faeces can be so distinctive it's possible to identify an animal species just from its poo! Every animal has its own special sort of poo, so this is just a small sample of a huge variety of different poos (some were just too big or runny to fit on the page).

8

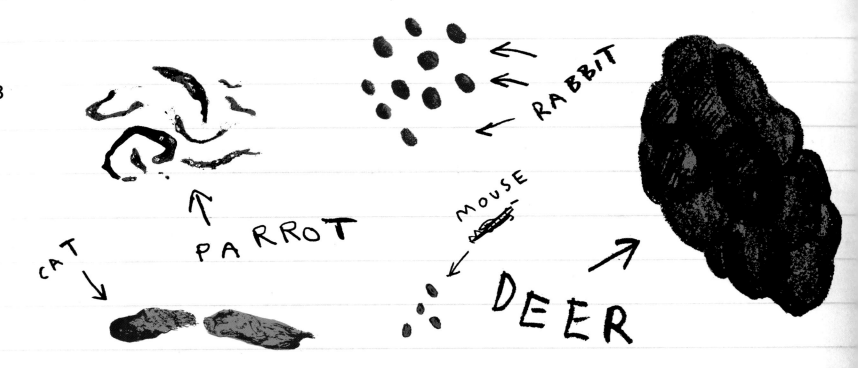

CAT

PARROT

RABBIT

MOUSE

DEER

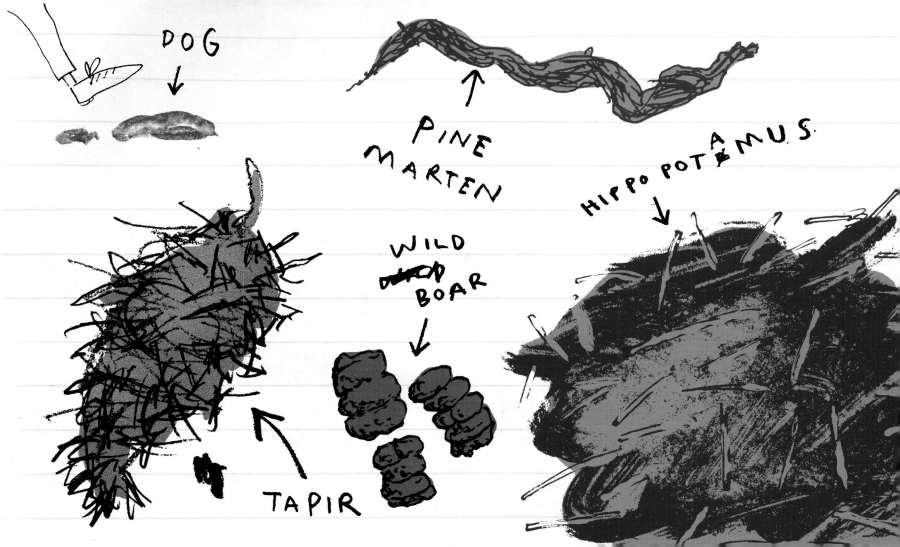

DOG

PINE MARTEN

HIPPO POT~~A~~MUS.

WILD ~~PIG~~ BOAR

TAPIR

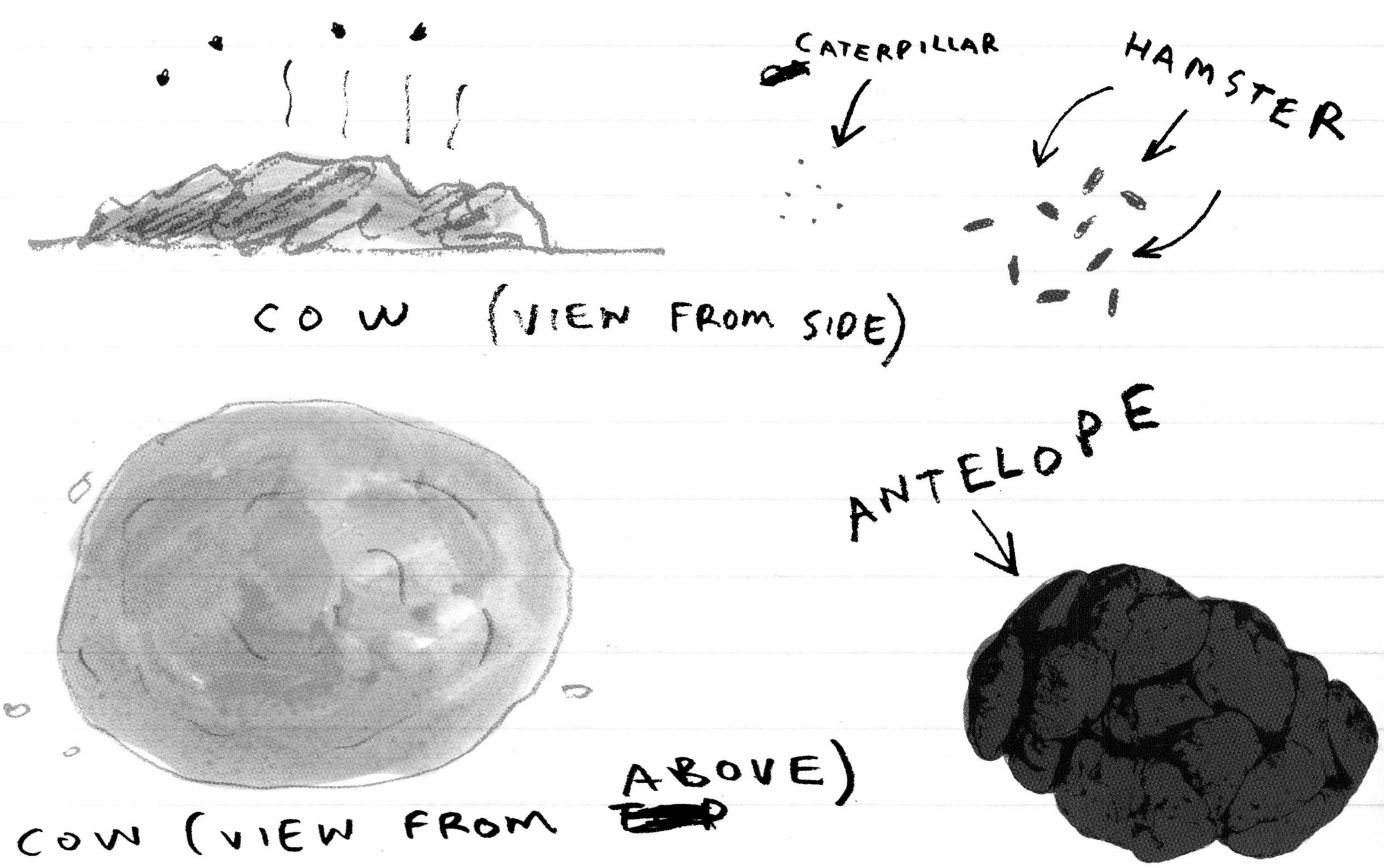

CO W (VIEW FROM SIDE)

CATERPILLAR

HAMSTER

10

COW (VIEW FROM ~~BELOW~~ ABOVE)

ANTELOPE

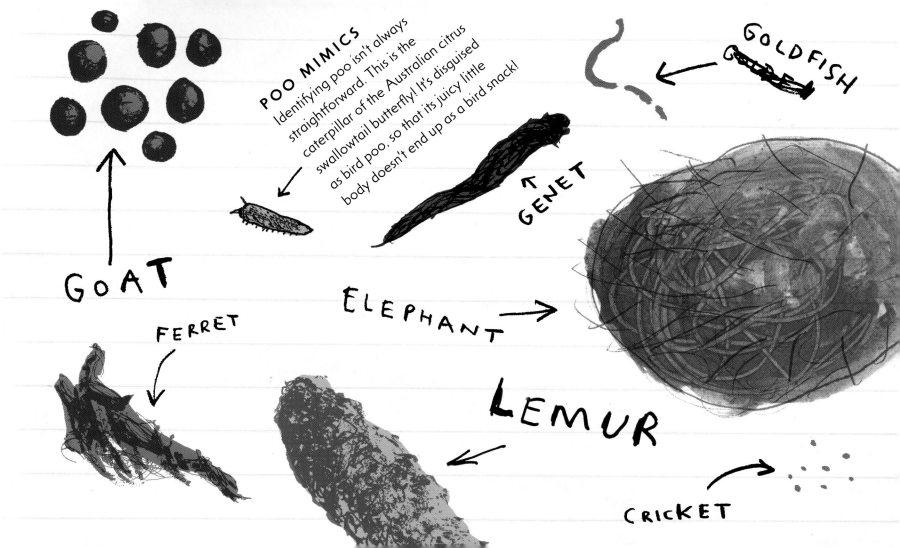

GOAT

POO MIMICS
Identifying poo isn't always straightforward. This is the caterpillar of the Australian citrus swallowtail butterfly! It's disguised as bird poo, so that its juicy little body doesn't end up as a bird snack!

GOLDFISH

GENET

FERRET

ELEPHANT

LEMUR

CRICKET

WHAT'S IT ALL FOR?

Sloppy or hard, skinny or fat, all this poo is doing something very important: it's the way animals get rid of rubbish — not drink cans and sweet wrappers, but body rubbish. What is body rubbish? Well, it's the remains of food that the body can't use, like worn-out blood cells, germs and other unwanted bits, such as worms that try to live inside the gut. As you can see, faeces can contain quite a few different things.

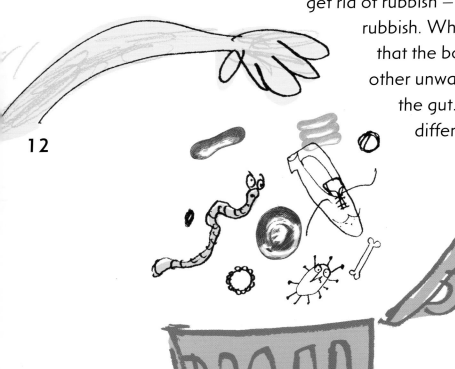

12

But mostly, poo is made of the bits that are left after food has been chewed, swallowed, mixed and mashed from mouth to gut and digested. And the reason that there are so many shapes and sizes of poo is that animals eat all sorts of different food.

Many animals also produce urine – wee, pee, tinkles, number ones. Urine is another of the body's dustbins and is made of waste from the blood dissolved in water. It usually comes out through a different hole, but some animals, like birds, squirt urine and faeces out together through the same one. Insects don't really make urine at all and just produce faeces that have their own special name, frass.

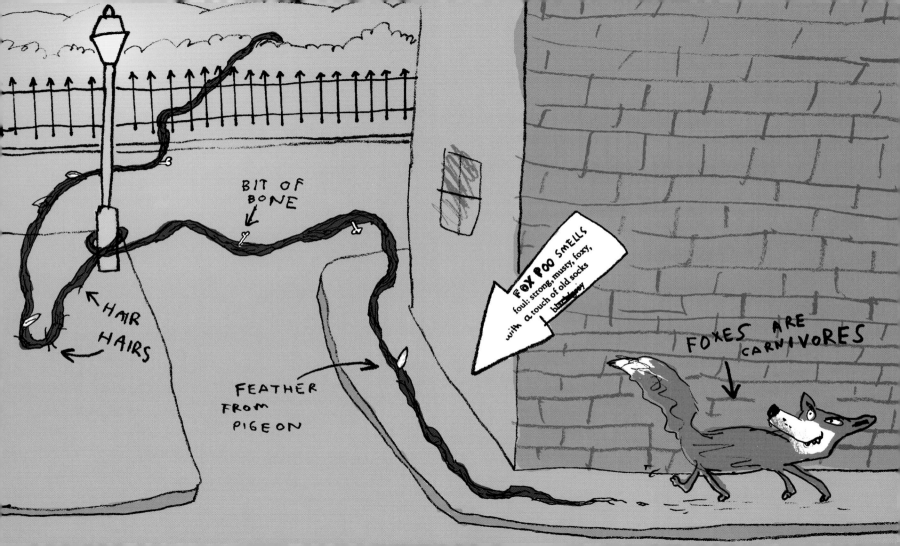

Meat-eating animals — such as tigers, lions and foxes — have faeces that usually look very different from those of plant-eaters. Their poos contain hair, fur, feathers, bone — in fact any bits of the animals they have eaten. These tend to bind the poo together, making it long and untidy.

But the biggest difference between the poos of meat-eaters (carnivores) and plant-eaters (herbivores) is quantity. Meat is a rich source of nourishment that's easy to digest, with very little waste. So carnivores don't need to eat, or poo, very often.

Plants are a lot less nourishing and difficult to digest, with lots of bits that are thrown away in faeces. So herbivores need to eat almost all the time just to stay alive, and they hardly ever stop defecating.

Sheep are herbivores

SLOPPY OR PLOPPY?

The other reason that poos come in different shapes is water.

Vampire bats obviously feed on blood (not usually human), and blood is mostly water. So they get rid of the water by producing faeces like runny jam. Camels are famous for their ability to go without water, and one way they manage it is by doing very dry poos.

But even animals that eat the same food have poos that can be very different. A cow produces about ten big sloppy pats every day, but a sheep grazing on the same grass produces hundreds of little round droppings like currants. Why? The answer is that sheep hardly ever drink, they get water from the plants they eat, so by the time the grass has become poo, it's pretty dry, and breaks into little bits. But cows love to drink, they don't need to take moisture from the grass, so their poo can be like thick soup!

A VERY DRY CAMEL POO

JUST Like Grandma used to make...

VAMPIRE JAM

16

DIAGRAM of SHEEP + COW ~~FEEDING~~ ~~GRASS~~

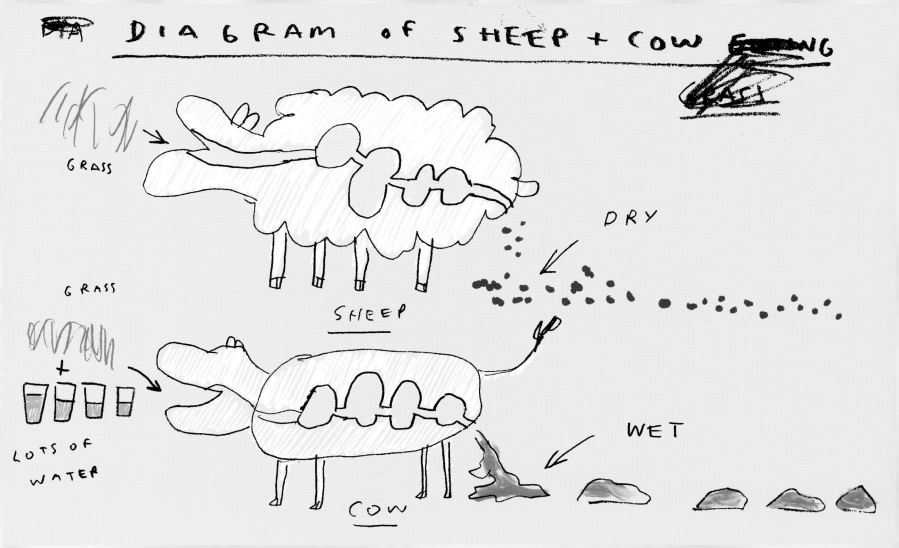

GRASS

SHEEP

DRY

GRASS

+

LOTS OF
WATER

COW

WET

RAINBOW POOS

The one thing that doesn't seem to vary much between different sorts of poo is colour. Most are brownish or blackish. One reason for this is that mixing all the different colours in food is like mixing all the colours in a paint box — you get a kind of dark, yucky colour. Another reason is that when a body digests food it breaks down some of the colours it contained, leaving it dull and greyish. When this is added to the dark brown remains of dead blood cells chucked out by the body, hey presto you get the familiar poo-brown! Bird faeces are usually the typical dark-yuck colour too. But their droppings are splodged with white, because their white and pasty urine leaves their body through the same hole as their poo.

19

Sometimes an animal may eat so much of a brightly coloured food that the colour gets through to the poo (as anyone who's eaten beetroot soup will know!). Birds feasting on berries in the autumn can have droppings that look like sugar candy — pink or mauve from the berries, and striped with white. Blue whales, too, can have tinted faeces. When they feed on pink shrimps — swallowing a tonne in a single mouthful — they do huge pink poos that look like giant blobs of strawberry ice cream breaking up in the water.

← BLUE-WHALE POO

PROBLEMS SOLVED WITH POO

Poo may be mostly the leftovers from food, but some animals – herbivores in particular – have such a hard time getting nourishment from their food that using these leftovers can help.

Rabbits, for example, simply can't get all the nourishment they need from their food unless they digest it twice. And the simplest way to do that is to tuck into their own faeces. First, bunny eats fresh green leaves or grass, which passes through its digestive system and pops out as soft, dark pellets of poo. The rabbit eats these, still warm, straight from its bottom, and the food gets digested for a second time. After that, bunny has got all the nourishment it can from its meal, so the next lot of faecal pellets are just waste, and are deposited above ground.

Koalas have problems digesting their food too. They eat eucalyptus leaves, which are tough, full of poisons and very hard to digest. The only way koalas can get what they need from their unappetizing diet is with the help of tiny microscopic creatures in their gut, called microbes, that do the job for them. But baby koalas aren't born with this band of tiny helpers, so the mother koala gives the baby some of hers – by feeding the youngster a little meal of poo, which is full of the gut microbes!

KOALA and BABY

CUTE BUNNY STORY

Many other herbivores pass on these essential digestive helpers when their babies eat food with an accidental splash of their mother's faeces on it. Baby elephants, however, sometimes want to be sure they've got their microbes, and tuck into some of Mum's poos on purpose! Just one meal of this kind is enough to get the tiny helpers into the gut.

Poo-eating — whether on purpose, or by accident — is useful to a whole group of other sneaky creatures, called parasites. Some parasites, such as tapeworms and roundworms, can live inside other animals' intestines, where they stay cosy and well-fed inside their host's gut. The worms also put their eggs into their host's faeces. The eggs get eaten with the poo and hatch out inside their new home.

Meat-eating animals occasionally eat plant-eaters' poo — just for the smell. Eating the faeces of their prey helps predators to smell like the animals they need to catch, so they can sneak up on them without their own scent giving them away. Pet dogs still have this habit left over from when their ancestors had to hunt dinner, instead of getting it in a bowl.

WHERE'S MY DINNER?

Predators look for useful clues about where to find dinner by checking out their prey's poo. Nice fresh poo can mean that food is close at hand. Baby animals make easy meals, so their faeces are like a sign saying "dinner is served". That's why some animal parents are careful that when they leave the home they get rid of their youngsters' poos, as they don't want predators to know that their young are "home alone".

24 Many small birds, for example, are incredibly picky about leaving droppings lying around the nest. After they've been fed, the baby birds obediently turn round, stick their bums up over the edge of the nest, and produce a nice neat dropping with a coating on the outside that acts like a bag. The mum or dad bird picks it up in their beak and flies off with the poo to drop it somewhere out of sight.

Most small animals have to watch out for predators even when they're fully grown. Golden moles from South Africa stay underground all the time because they are just about snack-sized as far as a bird of prey or a jackal is concerned. But the moles don't want to have faeces all over their homes, so they keep one little chamber in their large burrows just for pooing in.

DIAGRAM SHOWING THE INSIDE OF A GOLDEN MOLE BURROW

TOILET TALK

Golden moles aren't alone in having a special place to poo. Latrines, as these animal toilets are known, are quite common in nature and used for a lot more than just pooing.

Giant otters, which live in big family groups in the rivers of South America, have giant latrines, and making and using them is a family affair. All the otters in the group trample an area of the river bank bigger than a snooker table until it's quite flat, then they poo all over it. The smell is overpowering, and the flattened plants on the bank can be seen from far up and down the river. The latrine isn't just a toilet, a place to defecate, it's a great big message for any new otter in town that says, "This is our river and there are so many of us that we've done all this poo. So you'd better get lost."

27

In fact, sending messages is what latrines are all about. Badgers, which also live in family groups, use latrines to mark the edge of their territory. They dig small pits and poo in them, leaving a smelly signal saying, "This is our patch, keep off!" Tigers and other big cats leave their faeces in special piles of earth, called scrapes, to say the same thing. Male hippos like to spread their message around. They quickly waggle their tails as they defecate, spraying poo, and its macho message about how big and tough they are, in all directions.

Latrines and poo in general can be used to send more complicated messages, too. A poo can contain all sorts of different smells. A quick sniff can tell an animal who did the poo, how old they were, what sex they were and if they were head of the gang or bottom of the pile! What's more, the strength of the smell fades with time, so it's possible to tell when the poo was done — today, yesterday or last week. All this can make a latrine into a kind of notice-board.

Peccaries, wild pigs from the South American jungle, live in big gangs. When everyone is busy finding food all day it can be hard to keep up with their social lives. They have a big latrine in the centre of their territory that everybody uses. And each time a peccary has a poo, it has a good old sniff of the latrine to find out what's going on in the group — who's around, who's pregnant, who's ready to mate, who's boss and who wants to be!

Rabbits are group-living animals which use latrines like notice-boards too. Any slight mound can become a latrine where lots of different rabbits come to defecate. With tens or even hundreds of rabbits living in a maze of burrows, a good sniff of a latrine keeps a rabbit up to date with what's going on.

Latrines can also be important for solitary animals, which sometimes use them as a "lonely hearts" advert to find a mate. Genets, small spotted catlike animals from Africa and Southern Europe, hunt and live alone. They have latrines in prominent places such as the top of a big tree, a high flat roof or a big rock. Any genet passing through the area is bound to find a latrine, and in one sniff it knows if there are any possible mates or likely rivals in the area.

Sloths have perhaps the most extreme latrine-using habits of any animal. They live solitary lives, high in the treetops of South American rainforests, where they eat leaves, leaves and more leaves. Unlike many other herbivores they don't defecate very often. Every four days a sloth climbs down from its treetop home to do a poo in its own private latrine at the base of a tree. The piles of dung at these latrines can be huge and very smelly, and as sloths don't see much of each other, checking out the pong at each other's latrine is almost the only way they keep in touch.

NAVIGATION BY NOSE (AND BOTTOM)

The lasting smell of faeces makes them useful to animals in many different ways. Hippos also use their poo for navigation, for example. At night they leave the rivers to eat grass on dry land, marking their trail with piles of dung. Even on the darkest nights the hippos can find their way back by following the smell of their poo.

33

WHAT'S HAPPENING TO ALL THAT POO?

A single hippo can add several kilos of poo to a signpost dung pile in one night, and yet the piles never get any bigger. And of course hippos aren't the only ones producing large amounts of faeces. All over the world, animals are defecating all of the time. Imagine all those billions of tonnes of poo!

What happens to it all? All sorts of things!

A small amount of poo gets reused for building! Millepedes make a nest for their eggs from their own poo, using the tiny pellets of faeces like miniature bricks. In Africa, oven birds, which make complicated predator-proof mud nests, use the dung of large animals like antelope, water buffalo and domestic cattle, especially when water is short and mud is hard to find.

35

Some termites use their poo to make gardens! Termites eat wood, which is so hard to digest that some species don't bother. They just chew it up and poo it out. Then they stick their poos together to make lumps, called "combs", and grow mushrooms on them. These mushroom gardens deep in the termite mound provide food for the whole colony.

Even humans have used poo as a cheap building material. Hundreds of years ago most ordinary houses were built from a mixture of mud and cow dung slapped onto a frame of woven willow branches. In some countries cattle dung is still used to help build houses, and burnt as fuel where wood is scarce.

PROFESSIONAL POO-EATERS

The real reason that we're not up to our necks in faeces is that one animal's poo is another animal's lunch. There are plenty of animals that make a living by feeding on faeces that aren't theirs, a habit that has the scientific name "coprophagy". Some of the most extraordinary of these poo-eaters, or coprophages, are the dung-beetles. Seeing them at work you can see how so much poo disappears so quickly. In Africa, within minutes of an elephant poo hitting the ground in a great steaming pile, there is a whirr of wings and the dung-beetles arrive and set to work.

Some dive straight into the dung and others tunnel beneath it and bury it. Some roll balls of dung away and bury them two metres under the ground. But all of them eat it, and lay eggs on it, and when those eggs hatch, the dung provides food for the beetle grubs. Within two hours, up to 16,000 dung-beetles might have arrived and there may be no sign of the elephant faeces at all.

There are 7,000 different kinds of dung-beetles all over the world, and they all have a particular sort of poo that they prefer. Some small species like the ready-rolled balls of rabbit faeces; others can cope with a large pile of cow or horse dung. Desert dung-beetles collect dung as dry and hard as concrete, and bury it deep in moist sand so that it sucks up water and gets soft enough to eat. Rainforest dung-beetles can climb about in the branches twenty-five metres up. They scrape monkey poo off the leaves then bring it down to the forest floor to bury it. These beetles are tree-planters, because monkeys eat tree fruits, the seeds of which come out in monkey faeces and get buried along with their poo.

Australian farmers discovered just how important dung-beetles were when they introduced cows to Australia. Australian dung-beetles were used to the dainty and delicate little poos of kangaroos and wallabies – they'd never seen cow dung before and couldn't manage those big pats. So the cow poo just sat in the sun, covering more and more land and giving millions and millions of flies a perfect place to breed. In some places there were so many flies that they filled the air and it was hard to breathe. Then in 1967 biologists brought dung-beetles that were used to big-scale poos from other countries and released them in Australia. The dung-beetles loved it, and soon the cowpats and the flies were disappearing from the Australian countryside. The people of Cootaburra, a small town in South Australia, were so grateful to the beetles that they made a model of a dung-beetle six storeys high on a hill outside the town so no one would ever forget how important dung-beetles are.

In other parts of the world, including Europe and America, there have always been large animals with big poos. So the faeces of horses and cows get cleared away by native dung-beetles and more than a hundred other species of insects. What the insects can't finish, worms, fungi and microbes can. Poo just doesn't stand a chance, and is used up in only a few weeks.

HOLY BAT POO

Not all faeces disappear so quickly, because sometimes there's just so much of it that the "clean-up" takes years. Fifty tonnes of poo falls on the floor of Bracken Cave in the southern United States every day from the bottoms of the 20 million bats that live there. Across the world there are many similar caves that are home to millions of bats, with floors metres deep in bat droppings. In some of them bat researchers even ski on the mountains of poo.

With such a huge food supply, it isn't surprising that there are many tiny mouths busily eating it. In one bat cave in Trinidad, researchers counted a million poo-eaters in a single patch of faeces the size of a picnic table. There were mites the size of pinheads and cockroaches as long as your little finger. All these coprophages made meals for other creatures: toads ate the cockroaches, and snakes and opossums ate the toads! No matter how much bat poo the coprophages ate, it never ran out because every dawn a new supply was delivered fresh by air! This makes bat caves such a good home that some animals never leave: Niah Cave in Borneo has a kind of poo-eating earwig and a species of earwig-eating gecko that are found nowhere else on Earth!

43

THE ONE and ONLY...

AND I EAT EARWIGS!

I EAT POO!

FAECAL FARMERS

Ants go one step further than just eating faeces: they actually farm other animals for their poo. Greenfly feed by sticking their needle-like mouthparts into a plant and letting its nice, sugary sap flow into their bodies. It's a diet that's very high in water so, as they eat, the greenfly are always defecating, and their poo is very like their food – a sugary liquid. Ants walk among the greenfly, stroking them with their legs to squeeze out the sappy poo, which the ants eat straight from the greenflies' bottoms.

44 We humans think that we invented recycling with our bottle banks and our collections of old newspapers, but nature has been recycling for billions of years, since life on earth first began. Poo and the living things that feed on it are a big part of that natural recycling, helping to break the remains of plant and animal bodies into smaller and smaller bits that can return to the soil for plants to reuse. This recycling happens very quietly and almost invisibly, but its effect is huge. Without it, life on Earth would stop very quickly.

APHID

POSTMAN POO

So plants need poo to top up their food supplies in the soil. But that's not the only job poo does for plants, it can be their postman too! Many animals eat fruits and berries and the plant seeds inside them. The seeds are carried from the parent plant in the animals' stomachs and pop out later in faeces, delivered to a new place where they can sprout and grow – which is exactly what the plant wants. In fact, many plants make berries or fruits that will attract a particular sort of animal *because* its poo makes the best postman!

In the tropics many trees and bushes have juicy fruits that hang clear of their leaves and are green, not brightly coloured. These are perfect for attracting bats, which have big appetites, need a clear flight path and, because they feed at night, don't find fruits by their colour.

After they've feasted on fruit, bats don't stop to poo but often do it while flying over clearings in the forest. This makes them perfect seed-deliverers, as they take seeds to areas where there are no plants to compete with. Thanks to bat poo, areas that are completely bare of plants can be covered in thriving young shrubs and trees in just a couple of years.

♪ POSTMAN POO ♫
POSTMAN POO
♫ POSTMAN POO HAS ♪ A BIG JOB TO DO...

THAT'S MY JOB!!

POSTMAN POO

In northern climates many plants have seeds that are spread by birds. Birds find food by sight and, outside the tropics, fruit-eating birds tend to be small. So the small bright berries of many woodland and hedgerow plants, such as hawthorn, holly and honeysuckle, are perfect to tempt birds to eat them, and carry away the seeds. The berries are green until the seeds inside are ripe and ready to start a new life. Then the berries turn red and sweet, as a signal to the birds that dinner is served.

Mistletoe is the cleverest plant of all at getting birds – and their poo – to work for it. The white mistletoe berries that we use to decorate our homes at Christmas are a favourite food of many birds, like thrushes, blackbirds and robins. They eat the berries, but the seeds of the mistletoe that come out in their droppings are very sticky and cling uncomfortably to the birds' bottoms. The only way a bird can get rid of them is to wipe its bottom vigorously on a rough bit of bark or a crack in a branch. This is exactly what the plant needs. The bird has, without knowing, planted the seeds in the place where they are most likely to survive, a crevice on a tree branch where the mistletoe plant can easily take root.

CHOMP!

POO DETECTIVES

Seeds are made extra strong to survive chewing and digestion, and there are other hard parts of food, such as bones or shells, that pop out in the poo as good as new. These can be useful if you want to know what an animal eats, especially if you can't watch it feeding.

Sperm whales hunt in the deepest water, up to 2,500 metres below the surface, where it is always cold and dark. At this depth the water pressure would crush a human like an ant, so no one can follow a sperm whale to see what it eats. But just before a sperm whale dives from the surface to these mysterious depths, it defecates and, if a whale scientist is quick, the poo can be scooped up in a net. The hard parts in the sperm whale's poo are horny jaws and teeth belonging to squid and sharks. By looking at them carefully, scientists now know that sperm whales can eat big sharks, and squid up to twenty metres long.

51

Sperm whale's poo

2500 m

Bats, too, are almost impossible to watch when they are out catching insects to eat. Luckily, insects like moths, flies and beetles have a hard outside shell made of stuff called chitin. So, tiny chewed-up fragments of the insect's chitin shell come out in bat faeces. You can see them under a microscope — fragments of wing, shreds of leg, scraps of head. With patience, these bits can be matched with whole insects to show which ones the bat has been eating. It is even possible to tell how many insects a bat ate by counting the numbers of insect legs or eyes. Bat researchers all over the world have used this method to work out what bats have been getting up to.

One study showed that a colony of just 150 big brown bats in America ate enough beetles in one summer to protect local farmers from 18,000,000 pest insects!

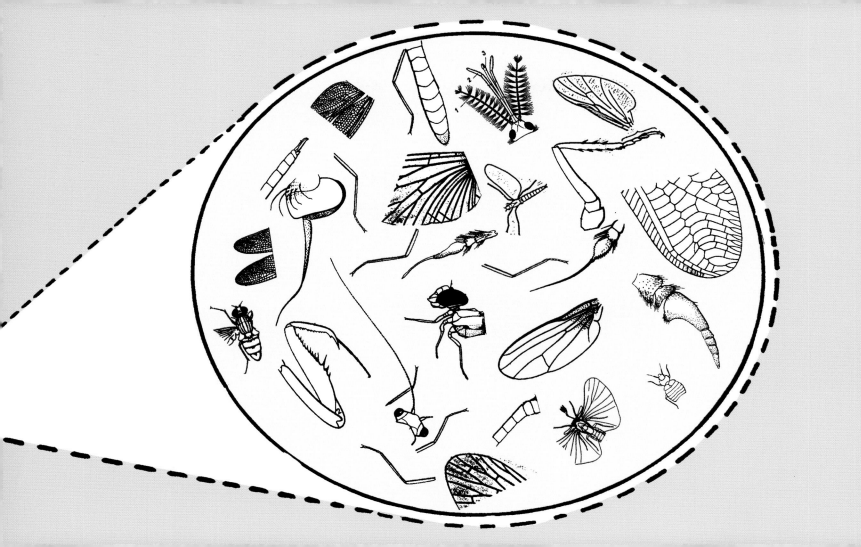

FOSSIL POO

Of course, the hardest animals of all to study are extinct ones. Nobody will ever see Tyrannosaurus rex eating its dinner, but along with fossils of its skeleton, T. rex has left some fossil poos (called coprolites). Coprolites found with a group of fossil T. rex in Canada contained fragments of

In a cave somewhere in Canada.

MANY YEARS BEFORE...

GRRRR!

AGHHH!

Triceratops ribs. What's more, the ribs had tooth marks that matched the T. rex teeth, showing that the big predators had slashed their teeth along the Triceratops' side, ripping flesh and bones. T. rex poo had shown not only what was for dinner 70,000,000 years ago, but how it was eaten!

MORE THINGS TO DO WITH POO

Faeces can be a great tool in the detective work involved in finding out about the lives of some of the most elusive animals. Otters are so shy that it's very hard to watch them in the wild, but they leave their droppings, or spraints, wherever they go. Each spraint contains enough of an otter's unique genetic code – its DNA – to tell exactly which otter left it, and also work out how it's related to other otters in the area. So by collecting spraints and studying their DNA, researchers can tell exactly who pooed where, and when. This shows how otters use their habitat and who is related to whom.

56 A much simpler method of working out who goes where can be used with wild animals that will take food that's put out for them by humans. Badgers and foxes are exceptionally greedy and will polish off all sorts of scraps. If the food contains a harmless dye, then all you have to do to work out where the animal goes over the next couple of days is find all the brightly coloured faeces. Good thing badgers and foxes are almost colour-blind, or they might worry about doing technicolour poo!

There are as many good stories about poo as there are kinds of animal. The ones in this book are just a small selection. As we've seen, poo can be used for food, fuel and building. It delivers messages, spreads seed and recycles nutrients to keep life on Earth going. Poo is probably about the most useful stuff on the planet. It's no surprise that a bird poo on your head is supposed to be lucky!

POO FACTS

Biggest: Blue whale. The biggest animals in the world do the biggest poos, 25 cm wide and several metres long.

Smallest: Bumble-bee bat. It weighs less than 2 g and does droppings the size of a pinhead.

COMPACT AND BIJOU!

Highest: Maned wolf. It has long legs and always defecates standing up, so it can leave its poo on objects a metre off the ground.

Smelliest: Orang-utans poo after they have been eating durian fruit. Durian fruit smell pretty bad to start with, so after they've been inside an orang and out again…

Weirdest: Mayflies, simply because they don't do poos at all. They live for just a day and don't eat, so don't need to poo!

INDEX

60

GLOSSARY

Carnivore a meat-eater
Coprolite fossilized poo

Coprophage a poo-eater.
(Someone else's poo, at that.)
Defecation pooing
Dung poo
Faeces poo
Faecal pellets poo
Forbivore a grass-eater
Frass insect poo
Graminivore a grain-eater
Herbivore a plant-eater
Latrine toilet
Microbes microscopic creatues
Number ones wee
Number twos poo
Omnivore eats anything
Parasite an animal or plant
   that lives in or on another
   animal or plant
Pat sloppy poo
Piscivore a fish-eater
Poop poo
Spraints poo
Urine wee
Vegetarian a human herbivore

61